a 7 week study
brought to you by p31 fitness

ISBN-13: 978-1721777723
ISBN-10: 1721777725

Book Layout by Evangela.com
Book design by Brenda Cicchini

Printed in the United States of America.

First printing edition 2018.

P31 Fitness
3960 FM 981
Leonard,TX 75452

www.p31fitness.com/worthit

TABLE OF CONTENTS

introduction

By Rachel Curtis, founder of P31 Fitness

The message of this book began over ten years ago in Garland, Texas, where I was serving as a youth intern at a church for the summer. I was a college athlete at a private Christian college with a perfect GPA, and former homecoming queen of my Colorado Springs high school. I don't give you these titles to boast, but to show you that I of all people should have been secure in my identity in Christ. But that summer, as I was working with 25-30 teen girls to help them discover their worth in Christ, I began to realize that I needed this message as much as they did.

I had led studies like this before in my dorm room and on weekend youth retreats. But this summer was different. My own struggles trying to earn grace through outward perfection came to the surface. That was the beginning of my path toward freedom, and my new quest to assure every girl and woman that she is indeed enough in the eyes of God - through Christ Jesus. It was also where the foundation for this book was laid, as I went on this journey *with* the teens I so desperately wanted to teach.

After college, I went on to teach and coach in Texas high schools. During off-season workouts at Sulphur Springs High School, I initiated "Wear them Out Wednesday," or WOW Day. After 45 minutes of intense workouts, I would lead the athletes in discussions of topics from the workbook I had created in college. Here I was in a 4A public high school, teaching the girls about their worth in Christ, and the strength and peace we can have through Him. As I gave them God's truth from His Word, I saw them begin to trust me. I was very straight with the girls about what they were wearing, who they were dating, whether they had confidence, and where that confidence came from. Self-esteem began to grow, girl drama waned, and the moms of my athletes took notice.

Toward the end of my first year at Sulphur Springs, the mother of one of my athletes asked if I would be willing to lead a summer bootcamp for women. I enthusiastically agreed. I created flyers and workouts and took registration. I was awed when 110 women showed up at the school football field for the first workout. This was the beginning of my business, P31 Fitness, high-intensity exercise classes for women with devotionals and Scriptures to help women understand their great worth in God's eyes. It has now spread throughout Texas, and is moving into other parts of the country. These classes are my main ministry for communicating the message that "you are enough" to women.

But that curriculum I developed for girls while in college and as a high school coach is still a message I want to shout from the highest mountain. So after establishing P31 Fitness, I also began leading weeklong summer day camps for girls aged 8-18, called Power Camps. Several P31 trainers have led camps in Texas and Arizona, and today, hundreds of girls have experienced the message that began with that Garland, Texas youth group. I believe that this message that "you are enough" is one that every girl needs to know, and it is best learned in community, with women mentors leading the way.

Some of the P31 Fitness trainers who have been involved with Power Camps have such a zeal for this age group that they wanted to expand upon the lessons and make it into a Bible study for teens to do with their youth groups, friends, or on their own. This book is the culmination of my work with high school girls that began when I was in college, continued when I was a coach, and developed more as I instituted the Power Camps. Three P31 Trainers, Stephanie Gugelman, Sherri Van Fleet, and Larissa Baker, have written lessons to go along with the Power Camp workbooks, and filmed accompanying videos.

FROM ALL OF US:

We are so thankful you will be joining us on this journey toward discovering our worth in Christ. Even though we are P31 Fitness Trainers, who teach this message to women on a weekly basis, we still feel this struggle at times!

But we have found so much freedom from the world's lies through P31 Fitness, that we want to start communities like it all over the country for girls like you. Even without the unique fitness environment of P31 Fitness classes, we believe that you can experience the same freedom if you hear God's truth about you within a community of girls seeking the Lord. You will notice as you read this book that the voices in each session are different, and the struggles the authors have experienced are not the same. Larissa, Stephanie, and Sherri are three very different women. Yet we have all found that within our P31 Fitness classes, we have a safe community of women, and those friendships have strengthened our faith and encouraged our hearts, regardless of differences in personality and ability. We have opened our hearts to our P31 classes, and to you in this book. We encourage you to do the same with the girls in your group; we believe this is so helpful in tearing down the walls we put up between ourselves, and allowing others to see our struggles and strengthen us with their love and encouragement.

Our heart for this entire program is to help women of all ages see themselves as God created them. As women, young and old, we can often feel like we are not enough. At different times in our lives, almost all of us have felt lost, broken, rejected, and alone. Then we seek love and acceptance in places that can never satisfy our souls. Through the course of this study, we will discover the precious woman God hand-knit together—YOU! He called, created, and crowned you, and He loves you just as you are.

A LOOK AHEAD

Each of this study's seven sessions includes a reading, discussion questions, a coloring graphic, journaling pages, a beauty tip, an action challenge, and an optional "Digging Deeper" section.

We believe that this journey to discovering your worth in Christ will require you to dispel the lies we typically believe about ourselves. So we encourage you to document those eye-opening moments when you realize that something you believed had been true is actually 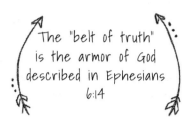 a lie. We've included graphics in each session for this very purpose. Spend some time praying for God to help you stop believing those lies, and truly put on the "belt of truth" . Also use Appendix A, Scriptural Affirmations, to find a biblical truth to replace the lie. Commit this truth to memory to continue to defend yourself against the lies of the world.

We also offer seven video lessons and a Facilitator's Guide, which includes topic introductions, insight to the girls' perspective regarding the topic, a leader devotional, and activity ideas for each lesson. Both of these are available for purchase on our website, http://p31fitness.com/worthit/.

Our website has many more resources available, including the message T-shirts worn in the videos, a Spotify playlist to coordinate with each session, and graphics to share on social media to promote this study.

We offer all these ways for you to engage with this study, not so you can find your worth in how much "extra" you do, or feel like a failure when you don't do "enough." You can do as little or as much as you like with this study. Whatever you are able to do that week- it is enough! You are enough!

We hope that throughout this journey, you will know God more and who He made you to be.

FOR SMALL GROUPS:

Before diving into the first lesson, we hope you will spend some time letting the group get to know each other, and building an atmosphere of safety, openness, and honesty. One of our goals of this project is to foster spiritual friendships among the participants, and mentoring relationships between participants and facilitators. The Facilitator Guide is a great resource to help the leader do that.

FOR INDIVIDUALS:

We are incredibly excited for you! You have chosen to go on a fantastic journey! Even without a physical small group, we encourage you to join a discussion of what you're learning about God and yourself through our social media groups, on Facebook and Instagram. Search @worthitbyp31fitness.

While you could easily fly through this book, we recommend reading this book over a month or two. You'll have more opportunity for growth if you are dwelling on these truths by focusing on one topic a week.

Here is a possible schedule to help you study and apply a topic a week:

- **Day 1:** Read through the text of the session (or watch the video). Pray and ask God what it is He'd like for you to focus on this week regarding that topic. Write it down in your journal pages. Look at the Beauty Tip and Action Challenge for the week.

- **Day 2 – 3:** Go through the discussion questions. This may take you one or two days depending on how much time you have available each day for the study. The journal pages will be helpful in responding to these questions on your own.

- **Day 4:** Turn on some music, pray, color the graphic, and/or journal about what God has been teaching you this week.

- **Day 5 (Optional):** Journal through the Digging Deeper questions.

Whether you are doing this study alone or with a friend or group, we will meet you where you are. Together, we hope you will come to understand that you are enough, you are worth it, and your worth is found in Christ.

session one →

finding your worth

God did not make a mistake when he made you.
You don't need to be anything more.

Have you ever thought, *I'm not as* _____ *as her?* Right now you probably know a word to fill in that blank. Maybe it's pretty, slim, funny, or smart. The list could go on and on.

The tragedy is that we actually believe those lies. We tell ourselves that we are not good enough just as we are. We tell ourselves that we need to be more of something. We begin to place our worth in those things. If we're honest, those things become the drive in our lives and the motivation behind all the decisions we make.

So many of us are trying to please or impress those around us. We want others to like us. We want others to think that we have it all together, so we do all we can to create that picture of perfection. The girl who compares her beauty to others wears more makeup. The girl who compares her weight to others stops eating. The girl who compares the amount of laughter and attention she gets changes her personality. The girl who wants to please everyone works hard to be perfect in all she does. We all have struggled with *that one thing* that we think will make us *enough*.

I have been there. I have believed those exact lies about myself. I've struggled believing that who I am, who God made me to be, is not enough. Believing I need to be more of the things I am not.

It doesn't have to be this way. The God who created you doesn't need you to be anything more than you already are. He made you wonderfully well. Not only that, but He made you just as you are for this very moment in time.

When you doubt your worth and compare yourself to others, think about this prayer, from **Psalm 139:13 – 14:** *"For you created my inmost being; you knit me together in my mother's womb. I praise you because I am fearfully and wonderfully made; your works are wonderful, I know that full well."* God created your inmost being: the very core of what makes you unique. Before you were here on this earth, God was knitting you together. He was molding all of the things that make you who you are; from your physical features to your passions to your fears to your struggles to what makes you laugh to what makes you cry - God planned it all. Let that sink in. You are wonderful just as you are!

HIS NO MATTER WHAT

It's one thing to understand that God made you well. But that truth sometimes slips away when life gets tough. Do you ever doubt His love for you then? Do you ever question your worth when circumstances are suddenly against you? During these times, we need to cling to this promise: *The Spirit himself testifies with our spirit that we are God's children. Now if we are children, then we are heirs—heirs of God and co-heirs with Christ, if indeed we share in his sufferings in order that we may also share in his glory* **(Romans 8:16 – 17).** You are God's child, and as God's child, a co-heir with Christ. Jesus came to this earth and experienced it as you do. He suffered with trials, and you will have trials of your own too. Life is hard. But Jesus overcame and is in heaven enjoying the glory of it all, and you can too. Studying and reading God's Word will help in this understanding even more!

CHERISHED AND CALLED

We are made well, and will suffer if we are God's children. We must also remember that we are chosen by God, set apart to be light in a dark world. The Bible tells us we *"are a chosen people, a royal priesthood, a holy nation, God's special possession, that you may declare the praises of him who called you out of darkness into his wonderful light"* (**1 Peter 2:9**). We are God's "special possession." I love the picture this paints. Can you think of some special possession you have? I like to think that I am not tied to many earthly possessions, but I do have a couple charm bracelets that mean a lot to me. I have had one bracelet in particular since my thirteenth birthday, and it is full! It has charms to represent all kinds of things I did as a teenager, from playing certain sports to traveling on various mission trips. It is my teen years to my early twenties in a bracelet, a symbol of all those cherished memories. It is incredibly special to me. Imagine if that is how I feel about a non-living, earthly possession, how much more does God value *us* as His special possessions!

WOULD GOD 'LIKE' OR 'LOVE' THIS?

The sad thing is that we can know all this in our heads, and and still find ourselves doubting in our hearts. To not care what others think about us is easier said than done! But we have to focus on whose approval we are working toward: men or God's. The apostle Paul questioned this very thing: *"Am I now trying to win the approval of human beings, or of God? Or am I trying to please people? If I were still trying to please people, I would not be a servant of Christ"* (**Galatians 1:10**). We want our focus to be on pleasing God.

Whose approval are you trying to win?

Today, we have social media, which makes the temptations of comparing yourself with others and judging by appearances even easier to fall into. As we post our pictures and status updates, we think: *What will others think? Will people like what I'm wearing? Will people like my new haircut? Will people like this picture and think I look good? How many likes will this get?* Or we see our peers' posts and think: *She has a new haircut, maybe I should cut my hair too. I could never pull that outfit off; she looks better than me. Look at her smile, she's so happy--why can't I be happy like that?* We can become consumed with the need to be something more.

Does God care about your haircut or your clothes, or any outward features? Here's what the Bible says: *"The LORD does not look at the things people look at. People look at the outward appearance, but the LORD looks at the heart"* (1 Samuel 16:7). Others may judge you because of your outside appearance, but God will not.

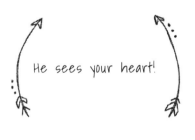

He sees your heart!

ME - VERY GOOD?

Are you beginning to see how God views you? Consider what God said after He had finished His creation. From the mountain tops, to the mighty waves that fill the deep ocean, from the vibrant blue sky to the bright stars that fill the night sky, God saw all that work as good. And on the sixth day of creation, God created man and woman. At the end of that day, Genesis 1:31 says *"God saw all that he had made, and it was very good."* Notice the words all and very. It does not say God saw some things He made as good, but He saw ALL He made and it was very good. Not even just good, but very good. **God did not make a mistake when He made you. You don't need to be anything more.**

Not only that, but you don't need to doubt this place and time God has chosen for you. He placed you where and when you are, gave you your family, your talents, and your appearance. We must believe this. Read this statement, with your name in the blanks.

God has decided that right now, at this specific time in history, the world needs a _____ and when He created _____ He declared that _____ is very good!

Do you believe this? It is okay to admit that you do not. It takes time to believe these truths. To be completely truthful, there are days that I do not believe this! Over the next few weeks, we are going to dig into these feelings of not feeling enough. Feeling lost and alone. Feeling broken and rejected. We will talk about the women God is creating us to be. Our hope is that at the end of this journey, you will see yourself as the beautiful woman who God created and know that you are *worth it.*

DISCUSSION QUESTIONS:

1. What does the world tell us about appearance?

2. How does God see us? Who are we in Christ? Use these verses to answer:

   a. Psalm 139:13 – 14: I am _____

   b. Romans 8:17: I am _____

   c. 1 Peter 2:9: I am _____

3. Now, how do you see yourself? (Take some time, be completely honest, and write down how you feel about YOU.)

4. Who should we try to please or impress? Use Galatians 1:10 to answer.

5. Do you find yourself looking at the heart of a person or the outward appearance? Why is this difficult for us?

    a. What does God look at (1 Samuel 16:7)? Which should we use to judge others: outward appearance or the heart?

6. How many times have you said, "I wish I were as _____ as her"?

    a. What are we saying about ourselves when we say this?

7. What are we saying about God when we say this?

Everyday when you look in the mirror
say something kind about yourself.

Key Verse:

Psalm 139:13 – 14

For you created my inmost being; you knit me together in my mother's womb. I praise you because I am fearfully and wonderfully made; your works are wonderful, I know that full well.

  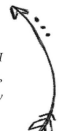

When you find yourself thinking "*I don't like who I am!*" Instead think, "*God created me and loves me in a way that I cannot even begin to fathom.*"

Dig Deeper:

Over the next few days, let's dig deeper into these truths that God has given us! Pick one of the passages from above (Psalm 139:13 – 14, Romans 8:16 – 17, or 1 Peter 2:9) and rewrite it in your own words.

Then answer these questions. You can write down the answers or answer them in your head. Just be sure to take time to really think about them.

- What makes the truth in these verses hard to believe for myself?

- What is one word or phrase in this passage that summarizes the truth that it holds?

- Have a conversation with God (pray) asking Him to help you begin to believe the truth that you've read about.

key takeaways

session two →

discovering your purpose

You do not have to be perfect to be used by God.

I've never been a confident person. I've spent many days and nights thinking back over what someone said to me, how I performed, how a conversation or email went, you name it. I replay it all in my head: *I should have said this or that. Why did I do that? How could I be so dumb? Wow, am I annoying? I am such a pain. I need to close my mouth. I wish I knew what to say. What are they going to think about me?*

The negative thoughts and questions would go on and on. With all this obsessive wondering and questioning, I would miss out on things in life. When I felt God leading me to step out in faith, I did not feel like I was the person for the job. How could I be? Plain, simple, ordinary me: the me who stumbles and is terrible with words. I was not confident in my God-given abilities to be the person He created me to be. I lacked faith in God's purpose and design for me.

What made it harder was when other people gave me labels, I would let them stick. It may not have even been something the person meant to be hurtful. It may have even been silly nicknames like Smurf or Ghetto-Booty. (Yes, both were applied to short, rounder bootied me.) A friend may have been joking around, and I would respond with laughter, but that was only a cover for the deep wound she had inflicted.

To add to the labels people gave me, I wasn't allowed to wear makeup or shave my legs in middle school. It felt like everyone else was doing it. I wasn't allowed to go out with people either, unlike all of my friends. To top it off, my curfew was a time more suited for a 10-year-old. I always felt like the odd one out.

There were many other things that everyone else was doing: simple things, like wearing designer clothes and hanging out at the movie theater. Then there were bigger, scarier things that everyone else was doing except me. I felt left out. Many times, I thought if only I bought a specific outfit or wore makeup, it would make me fit in. If only I could be like everyone else, maybe that would make me feel confident.

SEEKING BEAUTY, LOSING CONFIDENCE

I soon found out that those external beauty practices did nothing for my self-confidence. A few years later, I began shaving my legs and wearing makeup. Once I started wearing makeup, I would not leave the house without it. I soon felt like I couldn't go anywhere before I'd spent at least an hour in front of the mirror. While everyone else was enjoying each other, I was often busy layering on gobs of makeup. To help you picture how much makeup I wore, my dad would say I had Venus flytraps on my eyes! No wonder it took me an hour! Being obsessed with my appearance caused me to miss out on so much. I wouldn't splash in the pool or jump in the waves because I was worried someone would see the "real" me under all that makeup. I became dependent on a "fake" version of myself - a makeup-covered me. I wasn't okay with just being myself.

It didn't end there. I felt this compelling desire to be a certain weight. I became enslaved to the number on the scale. I would weigh myself daily, oftentimes multiple times a day, and that number determined how I felt that day. It determined how I saw myself in the mirror. The lies and nicknames I believed about myself, as well as the number on the scale, were things that affected what I saw when I looked in the mirror. Have you been there?

How much of my life did I waste being obsessed with my appearance?! *Why was I not content just being me?*

FREE AT LAST

The freedom-giving truth I finally discovered is that God made me who I am. He made the short, curvy woman who doesn't always have the right words, but who is a passionate visionary who can encourage others. He created not just external qualities, but the good works I would do in the world. Becoming the woman He needs me to be makes me His masterpiece.

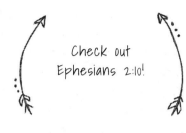

Check out Ephesians 2:10!

You do not have to be perfect to be used by God. You do not need to have the perfect words to speak truth and grace; you do not have to have a beautiful face and a cute body to be kind to others; you do not have to be the best at every sport and get the highest grades to be faithful to God.

We must move away from the world's idea of self-confidence and toward the better state of God-confidence. Rather than pursuing outward perfection, we must pursue our God-given purpose.

My quest for perfection made me struggle with doubts, fears and weakness in many ways, but God tells us that in our weakness He is strong. When we don't feel like we're enough, when we are hurt by what others say about us, when we don't believe we have what it takes, or when we struggle with poor self-image, we can turn to God for the strength and confidence that we need.

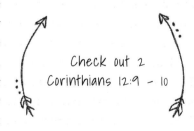

Check out 2 Corinthians 12:9 - 10

GOD-CONFIDENCE

I know that it is easier said than done. Finding our purpose takes dedication. It takes trusting his Word and what it says about us to believe His purpose for us. It takes not listening to the lies of this world to have God-confidence. I hope this study will lead you to see yourself the way God does: as His precious, beloved child, with an important job to do - probably *many* important jobs!

There is freedom in being uniquely you because of who He says you are: His holy and beloved child. I finally gained confidence in knowing who I was in Christ and became the child who would go jump and splash in the waves; 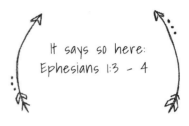 who no longer felt such a need to put on gallons of mascara before walking out the door.

It says so here: Ephesians 1:3 - 4

Mean girls may stand out and wallflowers escape the spotlight, but you were meant for neither of these. You were meant to trust in God's purpose and plan for you. He designed you to be a certain height - maybe you are like me and the size of a Smurf! Or maybe you were given a round lower half, and also the nickname Ghetto-Booty. So what? Short girls with rounder booties can serve the Lord with their unique gifts and abilities just as well as long-legged girls with huge grins, or average-height girls with naturally wavy hair.

FORGET PERFECTION

So when someone tries to hurt you or define you with a label, you can rely on His strength and walk confidently in His purpose for you. Or when you begin hearing Satan's lies about how imperfect you are, you can be strong in the Lord and ignore them. You have to stop seeking perfection and start loving yourself as the woman God created you to be!

Regardless of what anyone has said about you, or lies you have believed in the past, know that you were *created on purpose* for a purpose.

You can only show others Christ's love when you are confident in who God made you to be. Maybe God is nudging you to do something bold. Do it! Be confident that God made you just as you are on purpose. I am going to say it again: **You do not have to be perfect to be used by God.** I know that well. We will never be perfect! He wants to use YOU - unique and beautiful YOU! We can step out in faith for the jobs He has given us because our strength comes from Him. We can be different and completely okay with that. That's God-confidence.

DISCUSSION QUESTIONS:

1. Do you FEEL confident?

2. Do you compare yourself to others? In what ways?

3. Why is this a problem when we compare ourselves to others?

4. Where do your comparisons to others lead?

5. Do you praise God for what He has done, is doing, and will continue to do in your life? (Psalms 86:12)

6. How does having confidence affect your relationships?

7. What does God-confidence look like in your life, versus self-confidence?

    a. Self-confidence – "An impression of oneself, either being favorable or not"

b. God-confidence – "Knowing, resting, and trusting in GOD's abilities."

8. In all of this, we need to remember that it takes time to gain God-confidence. How do we pursue God-confidence each day?

   a. Proverbs 3:5 – 6:

   b. Romans 8:28:

   c. 1 Timothy 1:12:

   d. James 1:5:

When you start to compare yourself to others, stop and be thankful for who you are.

Key Verse:

2 Corinthians 12:9 – 10

But he said to me, 'My grace is sufficient for you, for my power is made perfect in weakness.' Therefore I will boast all the more gladly about my weaknesses, so that Christ's power may rest on me. That is why, for Christ's sake, I delight in weaknesses, in insults, in hardships, in persecutions, in difficulties. For when I am weak, then I am strong.

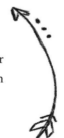

Use a dry erase marker to write your favorite verse from this session on your mirror.

Dig Deeper:

Reflect upon some of the things that have been said to you that have been hurtful. Maybe they are things that you say to yourself. Now look up Romans 8:31, and write it down in your own words.

Is there someone in your life who you feel is up against you? Perhaps there's more than one person. Read the verse from your journal again. If God has loved you enough to send Jesus to earth, if He loves you enough to have created unique, awesome you, then who could possibly be against you? No one!

Write down three things that make you unique and different. How can these things be used to make a difference for someone else? Use your "powers" for good! Use those things that make you stand out to make a difference for God.

created with a
PURPOSE

key takeaways

session three

becoming strong in the Lord

Looking to God for strength through changes,
both outside and inside of me.

Growing up, I was not a fan of change. The very idea of change still challenges me today. I like being comfortable; I like routine; I like for things to stay the same. When things change, you have to adapt and change as well, and that is never easy. Change comes in many different forms. It can be gradual, as with growing up, or sudden, like when you switch schools or move. It can be traumatic, like with divorce or death, or happy, like when you try something new or begin a new friendship. Change is hard, but I have come to understand that change can also be good.

As a junior high student, I moved to two different schools in two consecutive years. I attended a private Christian school from kindergarten through fifth grade, and then we switched to a public school. Not only did I face the normal middle school challenges of making all new friends and adjusting from one teacher to many, I also went from being in a church-like bubble to being out in the world. Over time, I grew to enjoy my new school. But then at the end of the school year, my parents decided to move to another town. I was devastated! I liked the school, the teachers, and my new friends. I even had a crush on a boy. Moving again meant starting all over again, and brought new challenges like finding a new church, joining new sports teams, and for this quiet girl, all that was completely intimidating.

Looking back though, it was one of the best moves for my family and me. The town where we moved became home. I attended school there from seventh grade until graduation, and have some of my best memories there. I made even better friends than before. I got involved in a church that led me to grow my relationship with the Lord and ground my faith. Through the youth group in that church, I was able to serve in many ways, including several stateside mission trips and one out of the country. I met great mentors with whom I am still in touch today.

LIFE IS CHANGE

I have endured so many more changes: Losing what I thought were lasting friendships. Making new friends. Quitting a favorite sport because a coach did not believe in me. Quitting playing an instrument that I loved to play because none of my friends were in band. Having a first boyfriend, and then breaking up. Choosing to switch colleges after my freshman year. Family problems. Getting engaged and then married. Moving across the country twice. Finishing school and then starting new jobs with each move. Finding new churches and friends at those churches. And my most recent change, having a daughter!

I would like to tell you that I have handled each change well, but that is not the truth. Some changes were smooth, while others were not. What is true though, is that in order to change, we need God in our lives. Whether we are changing schools or need a change in character, we need God's guidance, discipline, and love to make it through. Every time there has been a big change in my life, I have learned that there was an inward change that occurred as well, and God was always at the root of those changes. Sometimes change is thrown at us like a curveball, but sometimes we recognize that we need to change on the inside.

CHANGE ON THE HORIZON

Up to this point in our journey together, we have discussed our worth and stepping into our God-given purpose. God may be tugging on your heart about some things that need to change in your life. It may be that you need to believe you are enough.

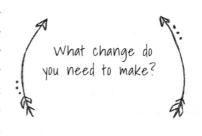

What change do you need to make?

It may be that you need to stop chasing what others think about you. It may be that you need to believe that you are great the way God made you and have confidence in that.

I have learned that no one can change our hearts but God. We can't change until we admit we need it. That is tough for me, because I am a pretty independent person. I was the girl in school who studied hard by myself, who thought I never needed help from others. In many ways, I am still that girl. With God though, this trait often becomes a problem. In my independence, I do not look to God as much as I should. I have my plan and usually just tell God the plan rather than ask Him what He has planned. When my plan fails, I become so overwhelmed, and that's when the waterworks start. Have you been there? It's hard to let someone else come in and direct our lives.

GROWTH MEANS CHANGE

If you want to live a meaningful life for the Lord, you must work hard to constantly change yourself for the better. Transforming into that godly woman will have its rewards, but it will often be hard. It may be scary or even painful, but when you receive your strength from God, He will help you persevere and achieve His goals for you. You can't do it in our own strength. Every one of us desperately needs God's help.

In order to change yourself for the better, you have to look to God first. **Jeremiah 29:12 – 14** says, *"'Then you will call upon me and come and pray to me, and I will listen to you. You will seek me and find me when you seek me with all your heart. I will be found by you,' declares the Lord."* You can't just go through the motions with God; you have to look for Him with all of your heart.

This turning to God must be a daily pursuit. Psalm 105:4 says, *"Look to the* LORD *and his strength; seek his face always."* You can't just seek God when you've run out of all other options; you need to do it *always*. Every decision, every day shapes you into the person you will become, and the impact you make in the lives of others.

PREPARATION FOR CHANGE

Sometimes the hardest part of change is waiting for it to happen. In those times of waiting, you need to build yourself up in our faith. **Jude 20 – 21** says *"But you, dear friends, build yourselves up in your most holy faith and pray in the Holy Spirit. Keep yourselves in God's love as you wait for the mercy of our Lord Jesus Christ to bring you to eternal life."* One thing is certain about this life: nothing is certain! God commands us to BE STRONG AND COURAGEOUS, but also reassures us that He is with us. He will give you strength to have more confidence, be kind, be wise, make good decisions, and be content if you allow Him to work inside of you each and every day. When you give your life to the Lord in full submission, He will give you strength for each moment.

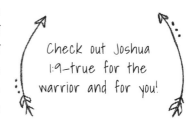

Check out Joshua 1:9–true for the warrior and for you!

DISCUSSION QUESTIONS:

- What are some things in your life that need to change for you to be a stronger person?

- How should you begin making these changes?

  - Psalm 34:3 – 7:

  - Philippians 4:6 – 7:

- Whose are we? (1 Corinthians 6:19 – 20)

- How will we become more like He wants us to be?

  - Jeremiah 29:12 – 14:

  - Psalm 105:4:

  - I Peter 1:15 – 16:

  - I Peter 5:6:

  - Jude 20 – 21:

- What are some qualities and characteristics that God wants us to exhibit?

  - Colossians 1:9 – 12:

  - 2 Peter 1:3 – 11:

- How do these lists make you feel about change?

- When life's changes become intense, where can we go for safety? What should we do?

  (Psalm 46:10 – 11)

Journal a change you have survived, and how it has made you stronger.

Key Verse:

Psalm 105:4

Look to the LORD and his strength; seek his face always.

Everyday, tell yourself you are strong in the Lord and in the power of His might.

Dig Deeper:

The first step toward change is realizing and admitting we need to change, and sometimes that is the hardest part! Often, we think of *all* the ways that we'd like to be better, and then get overwhelmed. As girls, we can also get overly focused on external change.

Pray and ask God to show you just one area on the inside that He would like you to improve. Maybe you need more patience, a better attitude, or to be more organized with your school work.

Once you know what you'd like to focus on, write down three ways that you can actually achieve this. Ask God to help you see opportunities to work on this particular focus. Finally, at the end of each day, write down how you've been successful at the new change. Don't dwell on the ways that didn't go so well, but celebrate the victories.

key takeaways

session four

keeping yourself pure

understanding I am worth protecting and cherishing

I am a hopeless romantic: I remember well those moments when my crush made eye contact from across the room and I could swear he could see right into my soul. Or when he walked me to my next class, even though it was on the other side of the school from his next class, and he would surely be tardy. When our fingers accidentally grazed and my stomach flip-flopped into eternity and I longed for it to happen again. This is my kind of romance!

In today's world though, these little moments are just not enough. The world tells us that love is a tongue in a kiss—which is honestly quite awkward. The world tells us that for young men to want you, you must show them what you have to offer them by wearing clothes that show them your beautiful body. The world tells us that you love boys by *doing* things with them.

The world is wrong.

MADE FOR MORE

We females have this longing to be loved by the men in our lives. In Genesis, the Bible tell us that Eve was created to be Adam's "helpmate." She was brought into the world to be his irreplaceable companion. It makes sense then that we, as women, would have an ingrained desire to please and help men. There is absolutely nothing wrong with that! We were made for an impressive purpose. For so many of my teen years, I had this obsessive longing for a boy to truly know me. I wanted him to know all of my thoughts and dreams. I wanted him to know things I'd never shared with anyone else. I wanted him to know all my darkest, ugliest thoughts. I wanted someone to know all of those things about me—the good and the bad—and for him to choose to love me anyway. Have you had similar thoughts?

Want to know something? It's a rotten reality, but that boy doesn't exist.

God does though. He knows your deepest thoughts and dreams and loves you. He knows the things you've never shared with anyone else and loves you. He knows your darkest and ugliest thoughts and He loves you anyway. As we discussed in Session One, He has *chosen* you. He loved you enough to die for you. Isn't that what we all want? We want the kind of love that would die for us—and we've got it!

Now, don't get me wrong. There are some amazing Christian men in our world, men who are full of love and willing to sacrifice. But the reason they love so fiercely is because God has asked them to, because God has called them to it.

When I was a teenager, I was often confused and I would roll my eyes at the idea of God being the "ultimate boyfriend." I hope that is not at all what you are hearing me say. God is certainly not a boyfriend.

Understand that God loves you more than any boy ever could. And that boys and men will let you down because they are flawed, just like us! That emptiness that we all feel cannot be filled by someone else: it can only be filled by God.

TRUE BEAUTY

So how does that affect the way we present ourselves to the world? Will wearing shortie shorts bring us that love we're looking for? How about showing off that amazing cleavage that God has given you? What about not being able to leave the house without makeup, without having your best physical self on display? Our bodies were made for so much more than all that.

There is a powerful description of an amazing woman in **Proverbs 31:10 – 31**. Verse 30 tells us, *"Charm is deceptive, and beauty is fleeting; but a woman who fears the Lord is to be praised."* I have come to understand that charm can be a form of manipulation. Physical beauty is not a true representation of who people actually are. It is our love for the Lord—and the actions that we take because we love Him—that will make us attractive. And it will make us attractive to the right kind of person: someone who values kindness, goodness, gentleness, and thoughtfulness. Someone who loves God as much, if not more, than we do.

PHYSICAL PURITY

There's another verse from **Proverbs 31** that I've hung onto for many years. *"She brings [her husband] good, not harm, all the days of her life."* I want you to think about that for a minute. How many days are "all the days" of your life? Well, it includes today and tomorrow and yesterday, right? It includes all the choices you make today. All the choices during your college years. For all of these days, we are asked to honor our husband. You most likely haven't even met him yet! So what you do today should bring your future husband good, and not harm.

What kind of impact does this have on you today? Think about all of the choices that you make that could potentially dishonor your future husband: Allowing other boys to look at your body because of the way you dress. Perhaps allowing boys to *do* things to your body that your future husband may not like so much. Or doing things *to* a boy that would make your husband wickedly jealous.[1]

MENTAL PURITY

In addition to keeping our bodies pure, God also asks us to be pure of mind. **Philippians 4:8** tells us, *"Finally, brothers and sisters, whatever is true, whatever is noble, whatever is right, whatever is pure, whatever is lovely, whatever is admirable—if anything is excellent or praiseworthy— think about such things."* We shouldn't allow our thoughts to be consumed with boys or making ourselves seem desirable to others. We should be dwelling on good, right, and pure things, things that are valuable and excellent in God's eyes. Not only does this include what you dwell on, but it also means what you put into your mind. Books and magazines, movies and online resources that allow you to think about and explore things that you should explore with your husband someday—this does not align with God's will for you.

EMOTIONAL PURITY

We can spend so much time being consumed by the wrong things. I know for me, so much of my high school years were spent dwelling on my perfect someone. God wanted more for me, and He wants more for you. Will you listen to the truth in Scripture, which is so contrary from the messages of the world?

Rather than the ideal boyfriend or husband dominating your heart, let *"Christ...dwell in your hearts through faith"* (**Ephesians 3:17**). When

---

1   You may have already done things with boys that you regret. You don't have to carry that regret forever—God is all about forgiveness. Turn to Appendix B on Forgiveness to read about it.

you are *"rooted and established"* in God's love, then you will be able to understand *"how wide and long and high and deep is the love of Christ, and to know this love that surpasses knowledge—that you may be filled to the measure of all the fullness of God"* (**Ephesians 3:18 – 19**). God can fill you up with His incomprehensible love, if you let Christ dwell in your heart!

And when it comes to the desires of your heart, the God who gave you that wild imagination wants you to use it for purity and goodness. You don't have to chase after your perfect future, because God promises that He can do more in your life than you could ever imagine. He is able. Will you let Him?

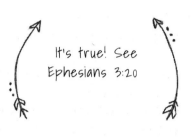

It's true! See Ephesians 3:20

SPIRITUAL PURITY

As God's daughters, we can't simply follow what is common in society; instead, we are called to a higher standard by God. We are not our own. Think about it: Without God's creation and without His sacrifice, we would be without purpose and without real, true life.

We must let our lives be intimate with God. Our hearts, bodies, minds, and souls were lovingly made by Him. We must learn to love and be loved by Him, surrendering to Him fully, all the way to our very souls. God desires to be first in our lives—always.

DISCUSSION QUESTIONS:

MODESTY

1. Use 1 Peter 3:3 – 4 to write a definition for modesty:

    a. To whom does our body belong? (I Corinthians 6:19, Galatians 2:20)

    b. Who chose us? (I Peter 2:9-10)

    c. How then should we treat our bodies?

       ◆ Romans 12:1:

       ◆ Romans 6:13:

       ◆ I Corinthians 6:20:

2. Do you show respect for your body in what you wear, in these different settings?

    ◆ Athletics:

    ◆ School:

    ◆ Worship services:

    ◆ Special evenings out:

3. When trying to decide if something is appropriate to wear, ask yourself the following:

  a. Is this going to cause others to talk negatively about me?

  b. Would I be comfortable wearing this around a godly man whom I respect?

  c. Would I feel comfortable wearing this around Christ?

PURITY

4. What does it mean to keep yourself pure?

  a. How do God's standards compare to the world's standards? (1 Peter 1:14 – 16)

  b. Use Scriptures to describe what it means to have:

    i. Purity of mind (Romans 12:1 – 2, Philippians 4:8)

    ii. Purity of heart and emotions (Proverbs 4:23, Matthew 15:18 – 20)

  c. Spiritual Purity (Ephesians 3:17 – 19)

    What are some practical steps you can take to fill yourself up with God's love?

  d. Physical Purity (I Corinthians 6:18 – 20, Galatians 2:20)

Get rid of TV shows and movies you watch and books you read that don't meet the Philippians 4:8 standard.

Key Verses:

Philippians 4:8

Finally, brothers and sisters, whatever is true, whatever is noble, whatever is right, whatever is pure, whatever is lovely, whatever is admirable—if anything is excellent or praiseworthy—think about such things.

Choose clothes to show off your personality, not your body.

Dig Deeper:

Have a conversation with God about your future husband. If marriage is part of His plan for you, He will bring someone into your life at just the right time for the both of you. Tell God that you entrust whether or not you marry, and whom you marry, completely to Him. Ask Him to guide you into trusting Him through the following activity.

Make a list of qualities that are important to you in a future husband. List as many things as you can think of, even if they seem silly, like height or hair color. Don't forget to include spiritual qualities like honesty and gentleness.

Walk away from your list for the day, and ask God to help you refine your list.

Return to your list. Add things that have come to mind since you last left it. Put a star on items that you know are important to God as well. Cross out things that maybe aren't so important now that you've had more time to think about it.

Continue to pray and pay attention to the men in your life. Look for qualities that you see are important in a relationship and those that are not. Refine your list as necessary, but don't obsess over it. This is strictly a tool to help you consider the things that God values in your most important human relationship. And it is an opportunity for God to mold your heart toward what He wants for you, too.

charm is deceptive

A woman who
FEARS THE LORD
is to be praised

PROVERBS 31:30

beauty is fleeting

key takeaways

session five

being loved

Receiving the great and personal love
God offers each of us.

We all seek love and acceptance. Whether your home life is stable or a mess, or your faith is solid or brand-new, it's easy to seek security in the wrong places. We might look for it in sports, academics, friends, boys, etc. We see fictional stories where love overcomes impossible circumstances to prevail. Watching the character win love and acceptance makes us happy, because we ourselves also have a deep need for those very things. Happy endings are part of the script, and that's comforting.

Love in the real world is a little different though, isn't it? Our love and trust is often tested, making it hard to know what love should look like or how we should love others. Maybe your parents have divorced, making you feel betrayed. Maybe a parent abandoned you and you feel alone. Maybe you have had impossibly high expectations placed upon you, making you feel like you have to earn love and approval. Maybe you are a foster kid and there is so much more to your story than anyone knows. Maybe you have had something unspeakable happen to you. All of these experiences can distort your view of love.

When I was a pre-teen, something no mother or father would ever want to happen to their child happened to me. A family member whom I loved and trusted touched me inappropriately. How could a grandfather do something like this to his young granddaughter? This experience shattered my entire family, making me wonder how I could love or trust anyone again. [2]

BRING ALL THE PIECES OF YOU

The broken people of this world can skew your view of love in a million different ways. We are all broken, because we have all sinned. You, me, your parents, your siblings, your friends, your mentors—every human on this earth. Here is the life-giving truth, though: the only One who can give us the love we seek is God in heaven. His love is perfect.

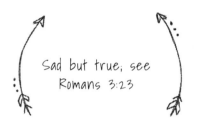

Sad but true, see Romans 3:23

My devastating hurt put me on a long and difficult road to understanding this truth. I was desperate to fill my heart and mind with other relationships and activities to distract me from what had happened, so I dove headfirst into my church youth group. I found everlasting friendships, ones that changed the course of my life. God even gave me a best friend whose sister had gone through something similar to me. These friendships were a key piece in Christ healing me from my past hurts. They were God's grace extended to me, making me rely on Him, not myself. Through my relationship with God, I was able to move on, to forgive, and to embrace His purpose for me. This all began with one sweet friend who invited me to go to church with her.

2   If you have experienced or are experiencing abuse in any of its forms (verbal, physical, sexual, psychological, etc.), please go to Appendix C for more information and resources.

WHOLE AGAIN BECAUSE OF HIM

I am who I am today not because of what happened to me when I was twelve, but because God saved me out of that brokenness through His church. I'm also thankful for my parents, who allowed me to dive into youth group. Through these people, I experienced the love of God, and began a trusting, open relationship with Him.

My story has become a reflection of the creation and the fall. In Genesis, God created all things, including man and woman. He gave them one command: Do not eat from the tree of knowledge. Guess what? They ate the forbidden fruit, committing the first sin. Because of this, all mankind now lives in this broken, sinful world. I experienced this, and so have you. We all mess up. We all make mistakes we wish we could take back. Because of this sin, we are separated from God, without hope. In the beginning, God had a plan for us to live in perfect harmony—in nature, with ourselves, and with one another. But that was gone with that one bite of the forbidden fruit. Depressing, right?

Here's the good news: God loves you in an unimaginable way. From the beginning of time, He was planning how He could spend eternity with you. However, to live in that perfect place, we need to be rescued, because we are not perfect. So God sent Jesus to rescue us, to take on our imperfections. **2 Corinthians 5:21** says, *"God made him who had no sin to be sin for us, so that in him we might become the righteousness of God."* He died on the cross to cancel out our sins. Compelled by love, Christ died on our behalf.

IT'S UP TO US NOW

Through my youth group helping me grow closer to God, I have learned what it means to give and receive love, and what it means to forgive. I chose to forgive my grandfather for his abuse. I even

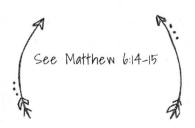

See Matthew 6:14-15

believe that if he has asked God for forgiveness, he has received it. As an adult, I still feel a little awkward when I see him, but I know that God calls us to forgive, or we ourselves will not be forgiven. Because God has loved and forgiven me, I can now choose to show love to everyone, no matter how deeply they have hurt me.

I can now see that had this event not happened in my life, I am not sure I would have gotten so involved in that youth group. I might not have accepted my friend's invitation. I know my relationship with my best friend probably would not have grown as deep had I not confided in her.

I honestly thank God for my past. I'm not justifying this act in any way, but I do feel it is all part of my story of God's grace. God has taken this horrible thing that happened to me and used it to bring glory to His name. It is part of who I am today, and it has allowed me to help others.

SHARE YOUR BROKENNESS

If something has happened to you, or you are going through something that is hard to understand, confide in someone. Keeping secrets will only make things harder. God isn't about secrets. He's all about freedom and forgiveness.

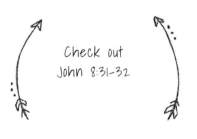

Check out
John 8:31-32

The story of forgiveness and love of God is for each and every one of us. I believe you are reading this book right now because God wants a relationship with you. You can find real love. It does exist, but not in the places you might have looked before. Real love exists in Christ alone.

Is it hard to believe that God loves you? Do you believe that God is your Heavenly Father and that He loves you and sent His Son to die in your place? Take some time to ponder that this week.

WHY ME?

Jesus came to make every bad thing untrue. He came to right every wrong, to heal every broken heart, to replace sadness with joy, to replace mourning with praise, to give us strength instead of fear, and to offer us perfect love. God wants to take your brokenness and create something new out of you. God has unbelievable things in store for those who love Him. **1 Corinthians 2:9** tells us, *"What no eye has seen, what no ear has heard, and what no human mind has conceived—the things God has prepared for those who love him."*

Jesus came to love us with a never-stopping, never-giving-up, always-and-forever love. He relentlessly pursues us. His love never wavers or weakens—it is perfect and constant. YOU are *loved!*

Let that sink in.

DISCUSSION QUESTIONS:

1. Is it hard to believe that God loves you? Why or why not?

2. Do you believe that God is our Heavenly Father? Do you believe He loves you and sent His Son to die in your place?

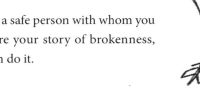

Pray for a safe person with whom you can share your story of brokenness, and then do it.

Key Verse:

1 Corinthians 2:9

However, as it is written: "What no eye has seen, what no ear has heard, and what no human mind has conceived"—the things God has prepared for those who love him."

God loves you in a way that no one else can. Accept His love and rest in it.

Dig Deeper:

Some of you are quite familiar with John 3:16. Even if you've never been in church before, you may have heard *"For God so loved the world that he gave his one and only Son, that whoever believes in him shall not perish but have eternal life."*

We've talked about this and I think you would agree that words matter. The spoken word and the written word carry a lot of weight. In general, the word "so" can mean "a lot" or "much," and we can often read John 3:16 with that meaning in mind. "For God loved the world *so much* that he gave his one and only Son, that whoever believes in him shall not perish but have eternal life."

But the word "so" in this passage has another translation in the Greek language (the language in which the New Testament was written). The other translation is "this is the way" or "in this manner."

Let's put one of the other translations into the verse.

"For this is the way God loved the world: that he gave his one and only Son, that whoever believes in him shall not perish but have eternal life."

Does changing the word "so" change the meaning of the verse for you? If so, what is the difference?

Have you ever had a friend or relative who tells you how much he or she loves you so often that the words lose their meaning? Sometimes if we hear that God loves us over and over again, we can become numb to the words. But remember that He didn't just *say* that He loves you, He *showed* you, through the sacrifice of His only son. And not only did Jesus die, He also rose again. This means we can have new life in Him. If you want to know more about how this works, read Jesus' full explanation in John 3.

- Do you have doubts about this act of love? (Doubts are completely normal!) What are some of your doubts?

- Talk to a wise adult who can help you answer your questions.

Ashley

Ash

loved

1 john 4:9

key takeaways

session six

receiving peace through prayer

Releasing all my questions and worries to Him.

Navigating this crazy world can make us feel like a rubber band getting pulled every which way. Do you ever wonder if you may snap under all the pressure? Between getting good grades so you can go to a good college, playing your sport well so your coach will get off your back, showing up for youth group and worship so no one will judge you, and of course, saving some time and energy for family and friends, how can you find peace amidst the chaos?

I felt stretched to the breaking point during high school. I played volleyball for club and school teams, and not only did it take up a lot of my time, but my coach had also cranked up her intensity level toward me. She was fine-tuning my playing so that I could reach my fullest ability, but it seemed constant and relentless. My play began to deteriorate. I began to pass terribly, so much so she told my parents to take me to the optometrist!

My grades were another area where I had to deal with being measured constantly. If my grades slipped, I would get incredibly frustrated with myself. My parents had always told me that if I was trying my best, then they would be satisfied with any grade. I just didn't buy that. If someone did better than me on a test or an assignment, I was furious with myself.

I was very involved in my youth group, but I would be late to church often because of volleyball practices or matches. My youth leaders didn't seem to understand all my other commitments - volleyball, school, family. They would kindly ask me why I was often late, if God was truly a priority for me. It was so frustrating—if this was the church, shouldn't they give me some grace?

THE SOCIAL MEDIA MAGNIFYING GLASS

Today, social media offers us even more ways to feel anxious to please others. After all, most people put the best version of themselves on the internet: the perfect nails, the beautiful bedroom, the cute-bedhead selfie. They only post the best moments of their day, not the horrifyingly frustrating parts of their day. Social media can be another pull we feel, ratcheting up the stress and stealing our peace.

Ever since Cain and Abel, bullying has always been a problem, and now we can add to that cyber-bullying. Being online allows people to make profiles anonymously and wreak havoc. It could be mean girls being wicked, 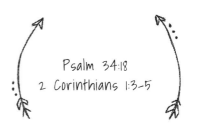 or just some kid who is so hurt that he needs to make someone else's life just as miserable. In either case, bullying can make its victims feel that life isn't worth living anymore. If you have found yourself in this situation before, I encourage you to reach out to God.[3] He is near the brokenhearted and crushed in spirit, and is the God of all comfort.

3   Please also go to Appendix D for more information and resources to help you through this difficult time.

When we have faith in God, we can rest knowing we were created on purpose and for a purpose. No matter whether we fit in or not. No matter whether we are part of the "in crowd" that everyone so desperately wants to be a part of. No matter what comes our way. We can have unbelievable peace.

THE SOURCE OF PEACE

It can seem like being busy and stressed are just inevitable in this world, but God does not desire this kind of life for us. He tells us in **Philippians 4:6 – 7,** *"Do not be anxious about anything, but in every situation, by prayer and petition, with thanksgiving, present your requests to God. And the peace of God, which transcends all understanding, will guard your hearts and your minds in Christ Jesus."*

Let's talk some more about what it means to come pray "with thanksgiving." Has someone ever handed you something, but as you grab it, they hold onto it until you say, "Thank you"? God just wants to know that we are grateful to Him, regardless of the outcome of our prayers. We have to be thankful that He loves us enough to hear our prayers. So as you approach God with the struggles and joys of your heart, make sure you are thankful for all He's given you.

Then you'll receive His peace. A deep contentment that you cannot find anywhere else, His goodness and grace will guard your heart and mind. It's like a spiritual force field! While the storms of life rage around you, they don't touch your soul. It doesn't mean that you will always be happy, but you can be peaceful. God commands us in **Psalm 46:10** to *"Be still and know that I am God."* We can only settle into this stillness, this forcefield, when we choose to be still and know who He is.

That peace comes through prayer, personal communication with God. The invitation from God for us to pray is an expression of His love and compassion for us. He doesn't want us to be pulled and stretched by outside forces. He desires us to live a life of peace, no matter what our external worlds look like.

BUT WHAT DO I SAY?

We cannot have that peace unless we go to God in prayer. God doesn't want to be a distant, vague presence in our lives. If we are in a relationship with God, it only makes sense that we would talk with Him. Imagine telling someone you love him, and then never talking to him. This is what we do when we don't take the time to talk to our Lord in prayer. When you spend time getting to know God, you develop a relationship with Him. You can also turn to Him when things feel out of control or when you do not know which way to turn. Remember He knows it all!

But how do we talk to God? Is there a right way? Are there specific words we're supposed to use? Do we need a special prayer voice in order to be heard? What about a special time or place to pray?

Think of Jesus as your best friend. There is no bad time to call or text your bestie. She'll read your text no matter who she's with and no matter where she is. And you don't have to guard your words with her; you just lay it out there. It is the same way with God. You don't have to wait to speak to Him. You can talk with Him anytime—in your head, out loud, in your bedroom, while you're putting on your make-up. He's available 24/7.

Remember, you don't have to impress God with your words. He wants to hear from your heart all the things that burden you. All of the things that excite you. All your joys and sorrows. One verse even tells us to "pray continually". That's God saying He wants us to spend every moment either talking or listening to Him!

See 1 Thessalonians 5:17

Does God actually answer our prayers? Definitely, but just not always in the way that we expect. Bill Hybels presents an interesting way to consider the way God answers prayers. He tells of a story where a pastor friend of his thinks about it this way (we've added the Scripture references ourselves):

1. No! — You are not asking for the right thing. (James 4:3)

2. Slow — What you are asking is not in my timing yet. (Isaiah 40:31)

3. Grow— You need to grow in some areas first. (Psalm 37:8–9)

4. Go — Yes! (Matthew 7:7)

DISCUSSION QUESTIONS:

PEACE

1. Does God care whether or not we have peace? Write down what He says to you about the importance of peace in these verses:

   - Isaiah 26:3:

   - Luke 5:16:

   - Romans 8:6:

   - 1 Corinthians 14:33:

2. How does God give us peace? Read **Psalm 46:10.**

   - Do you make time to do this, everyday?

   - How can you reserve 10 minutes to spend time with the Lord each day?

- What kind of impact do you think that will make on your life?

3. Is peace automatically given to you when you attend worship services or read your Bible? What do we need to do in order to receive peace?

   - Psalm 34:14:

   - Isaiah 30:15:

   - Colossians 3:15:

   - Philippians 4:6 – 7:

PRAYER

4. When was the last time you sat down and truly had a conversation with the Lord? What did it look like?

5. What can you change in your life to make this happen more often?

6. Here are some Scriptures to guide you into understanding how we should approach God. Write down what you learn about how to pray beside each of them.

   - Matthew 6:5 – 8:

   - Luke 11:9 – 10:

   - Romans 8:26 – 27:

   - James 1:5 – 7:

7. Here are some things God tells us He wants to hear from us. Write down the "talking points" you see in each verse.

    ◆ Matthew 9:37 – 38:

    ◆ Ephesians 5:20:

    ◆ Hebrew 4:1:

    ◆ James 1:5:

    ◆ James 5:13:

    ◆ 1 John 1:9:

8. What does prayer look like in your life? Is it personal and daily?

9. What is the point of prayer if God already knows what is in our hearts?

Pray the prayer below out loud, either with your group altogether or alone in a quiet place. Discuss which part of the prayer is most meaningful to you.

"Father, when you were on the earth, you prayed. You prayed in the morning, you prayed at night, you prayed alone, you prayed with people. In your hours of distress, you retreated into times of prayer. In your hours of joy, you lifted your heart and hands to the Father in prayer. Help us to be more like you in this way; help us to make prayer a priority in our daily lives."

When you wake up in the morning, begin your day on your knees in prayer to God. Be sure to listen and be still, too!

Key Verse:

Philippians 4:6 – 7

Do not be anxious about anything, but in every situation, by prayer and petition, with thanksgiving, present your requests to God. And the peace of God, which transcends all understanding, will guard your hearts and your minds in Christ Jesus.

Plan a time every day this week to spend some quiet time with God in the Bible and in prayer.

Digging Deeper

Look up Colossians 3:15. Write out the verse here. Underline two words: "rule" and "called." Your Bible may have different words, but find the synonyms for these words and underline them.

What does is mean for something to rule in your heart?

What does is mean to be called to something?

Now that you've considered what these words truly mean, re-read the verse and think about the impact of these words. Not only does God want you to have peace, He expects you to seek after it. It is your calling!

Finally, look up Isaiah 9:6. We typically hear this verse around Christmas time because it's a prophecy about Jesus. List the four names of God from this verse.

1. _____

2. _____

3. _____

4. _____

One of those names is "Prince of Peace." Jesus is the *Prince of Peace*. He can bestow it upon anyone who needs it and seeks it! He is so powerful.

Look at the other names on your list. This is the God to Whom you pray. Try using these names when you pray to Him.

Write out a prayer to God. Start out by thanking Him for at least two things in your life. Then write about anything that is plaguing your heart. If nothing is bothering you, praise Him for that! Then, pray for someone in your life who needs some peace and encouragement. Finish your prayer by asking Him to show you someone else in your life who needs you to pray for them.

be still

key takeaways

session seven

cultivating a servant heart

Overcoming the busy disease to love others right where they are.

We hope and pray that you are now on your way to finding your worth in the Lord and discovering your purpose in Him. We hope you understand the great importance of keeping

yourself pure, and how you can become strong through challenge and change. We want you to receive God's love, and to receive peace through prayer. Lastly, we want you to use all you have learned to love others as God loves.

But what does that look like, to love others the way God wants us to?

When I was a teenager, my favorite verse was **Jeremiah 29:11**, *"For I know the plans I have for you," declares the Lord, "plans to prosper you and not to harm you, plans to give you hope and a future."* I was and still am a planner. I would wonder about my future and sometimes genuinely worry about it. I would ponder, "What classes should I take? Should I play this sport? Should I date this guy? What does God want me to do in life? What is His will for my life? Where should I go to college? What will I do after that? I thought all of these questions were important to what God's plan was for my life and my mission as a follower of God. But as I have grown, I have come to realize that all of those things are ultimately about one person: me.

LOOKING BEYOND YOURSELF

Jesus tells us in **Matthew 22:37** that the most important commandment is to *"love the Lord your God with all your heart and with all your soul and with all your mind."* And the second most important commandment is to love your neighbor as much as you love yourself. That's it! We are called to LOVE!

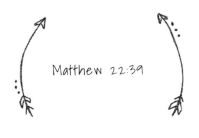

Matthew 22:39

How do you love others? We first have to know and believe that God loves us. You cannot love others without first understanding God's unwavering and unconditional love for you. When you accept and rest in God's love for yourself, you can begin to love others with the love of God. When you know you are enough because God loves you and Jesus saved you from death, you will be able to love others with a servant's heart. Once you understand and embrace this love, you can love others right where you are and right where they are—in your school, on your sports team, in your theater club, in your house, in your church. No worries or planning needed; just loving God and others. **Colossians 3:23** says, *Whatever you do, work at it with all of your heart, as working for the Lord, not for men.* While working with all your heart for the Lord, you will find ways to serve people.

THE SACRIFICE OF SERVICE

Being a servant isn't always the most glamorous thing and often requires sacrifice. Having a servant heart and putting others first requires discomfort and sometimes putting aside your own desires. But God sees the sacrifices we make and they please Him.

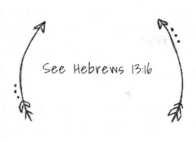

See Hebrews 13:16

Not only that, but He equips you to do good by giving you gifts and talents to use in your serving. **1 Peter 4:8 – 11** says that you are to use the gifts you have to serve others and give God's grace to others. What kinds of things do you LOVE to do? What are you good at? What brings joy to your life? These are gifts from God that you can use for His glory. When you understand you are enough and you have a purpose, you can begin to serve others. You do not have to travel far or be a missionary: you can put your passions to work right where you are.

LOVING THOSE WHO ARE HARD TO LOVE

What about the people who are hard to love? Those who are mean to you or laugh at you or just drive you crazy because they only care about themselves. It is hard to serve an annoying sibling. It is hard to serve that coach or parent or teacher who just never seems to be pleased with your performance. It is hard to serve the friend who betrayed you, or the enemy who belittles you. Putting on a servant heart requires sacrifice. God wants us to do good to ALL people, and Jesus even commanded us to do good for those who hate us!

That's a tough one! It's in Luke 6:27

A WOMAN OF WORTH IS A SERVANT

Throughout this journey toward discovering your worth, we've explored how God is shaping your character. We are all a **work in progress**. Philippians 1:6 tells us that God began a good work in you, and He promises to finish it. But we have our own work to do! Now it is time to fully embrace the woman of God you are meant to be. We see a wonderful example in **Proverbs 31:10 – 31**. Here is a woman who works hard to serve her family and household. She makes clothes for her family and prepares food for her servants. Not only does she serve those in her house, she also "opens her hands to the poor and extends her hands to the needy" (v. 20). Selfless service is the legacy you will lead as you mature into the godly woman God desires you to be.

So, delight in the exciting opportunities that the Lord has set before you to serve others. Don't wait. There is no time in your life more perfect than now to help others.

DISCUSSION QUESTIONS:

1. What does it mean to be a servant? (1 John 3:18)

2. Who are we to serve?

    ◆   Matthew 25:31 – 40:

    ◆   Galatians 6:9 – 10:

3. Why do we serve?

    ◆   Hebrews 13:16:

    ◆   James 2:14 – 20:

4. How should we serve? What should our attitude be?

   ◆ Rom. 12:9 – 12:

   ◆ Ephesians 6:7 – 8:

   ◆ Philippians 2:14 – 18:

   ◆ I Peter 4:8 – 11:

5. What about when we do not feel like serving?

   ◆ I Corinthians 15:58:

   ◆ 2 Thessalonians 3:13:

6. Why is it sometimes hard to serve others?

7. What is our reward for serving others? (I Timothy 6:17 – 19)

What are you passionate about in life? What talents do you feel God has blessed you with to help others? List the ways in which you can use those talents to serve.

Key Verse:

Matthew 22:35 – 39

One of them, an expert in the law, tested him with this question: "Teacher, which is the greatest commandment in the Law?" Jesus replied: "'Love the Lord your God with all your heart and with all your soul and with all your mind.' This is the first and greatest commandment. And the second is like it: 'Love your neighbor as yourself.'"

If your heart nudges you toward someone in need, act right then—don't wait. You never know what that person may be going through at that time.

Dig Deeper:

One of the most difficult things about being a servant is making your life available to others. When a need arises that you haven't planned to meet, and meeting that need will disrupt your life—that's when true servants are set apart from the ones who give to make themselves feel and look good. It's not the easy acts of generosity that will make us a servant—it's the hard stuff. It's serving those who are tough to serve, with acts that make us uncomfortable, and sacrifices that are inconvenient, with no rewards or recognition expected.

Read the prophecy in Matthew 25:34 – 40.

- ◆ Verse 34 tells us that certain people were blessed. What did they do that brought them blessings?

- ◆ What do they receive because of what they had done? (v. 34)

- ◆ These people are confused because they don't remember serving the King. How had they served the King?

Blessings or rewards shouldn't be what motivates us to help others. Our service will be the natural outflow of our love for others and our love for God. Pray for God to open your eyes to the ways you can serve "the least of these" in your life.

One of the fun ways to help someone is to do it in secret. Everyone doesn't need to know that you've done a good thing. You know and God knows and that should be enough.

work in PROGRESS

key takeaways

reflect AND respond

How should I react to what I've learned?
Can I move toward a better understanding of who I am?

What a journey we've been on together! As humans, our lives are an unpredictable mix of love, joy, hurt, sorrow, excitement, longing, and challenges. God never promises us an easy life. His apostles all experienced hardship after Jesus ascended. Paul spent many years in prison for preaching God's truth and love. But God does promise us that He will never let us down or abandon us! Isn't that a wonderful thought?

See Deuteronomy 31:6

Have you ever done that trick at a slumber party where one of your friends lays down and everyone else circles around her? You all put just two fingers from each hand under her, you count to three, and then lift her off the ground! It seems like she's floating! In actuality, you have all lifted just a piece of the weight.

This is what life is like with God, as we allow His work in our lives. He also gave us a family of faith- the Church! Not some building with a cross on its roof, but a group of people who love God, follow God, and who are on a similar journey to learning more about Him.

Know that you are not alone! Find a church family where you can dig in, serve, and study the Bible with others. Find a place to connect with people who will encourage you in your walk with Christ. A family that seeks truth from God's word.

As this book comes to a close, let's spend some time reflecting upon all that you've learned.

- List the top five things that you've learned through this study.

- In what ways do you need to change in order to become a more godly woman? Can you achieve this change on your own?

- If God loves us as we are, why do we need to change and grow? Read 2 Peter 1:5-8 to help you answer this question.

- What are three practical things that you can do today that will have an impact on moving toward a more mature you?

We hope that this study has helped you discover **your worth in Christ alone.** Through this journey, we hope that you will take the truths you have learned from God's Word and keep them close to your heart for the days when you don't feel like you are enough. We pray that this study has deepened your relationship with the Lord or perhaps led you to start a relationship with Him. We pray that you know that you are His beloved, precious daughter whom He created on purpose and for a purpose. You are chosen. You are called. You are enough. You are worth it!

appendix

Appendix A

Forgiveness

Have you done something that you regret? A regret that consumes you? A guilt that you carry around with you everywhere you go?

Let me tell you, this is not what God wants for you.

Romans 8:35, 37 – 39 says "Who shall separate us from the love of Christ? Shall trouble or hardship or persecution or famine or nakedness or danger or sword? ...

There is NOTHING that you can do that will separate you from His love. NO. THING. You might think, "Well, you don't know what I've done." I don't have to know! What I do know is that He loves you.

It is grace that saves us, not anything any of us have done or can do. *Ephesians 2:8 – 9 says "For it is by grace you have been saved, through faith--and this is not from yourselves, it is the gift of God—not by works, so that no one can boast."*

Grace is being given something that you don't deserve. Even though we don't deserve His love —not any one of us—He gives it to us anyway. He gets to show us how powerful He is through His forgiveness.

One of the best pictures we have of God's forgiveness is in Luke. session 23 tells us the story of Jesus' death on the cross. Next to Him hung two criminals. We don't know what they did, but we know their crimes were worthy of crucifixion. While suffering there next to Jesus, one criminal mocked Jesus, but the other said,

"We are punished justly, for we are getting what our deeds deserve. But this man [Jesus] has done nothing wrong." Then he said, "Jesus, remember me when you come into your kingdom." Jesus answered him, "Truly I tell you, today you will be with me in paradise." (vv. 41–43)

The criminal knew that his deeds meant he deserved death, just as you need to let God know that you understand that your wrong choices separate you from Him. If this criminal can be forgiven because of his faith in Jesus, can't you also be forgiven? All you have to do is ask God for forgiveness. Let Him know that you need His love to cover your wrong choices. Once you've asked for forgiveness, He has forgiven you. You don't have to keep asking for forgiveness for the same wrong decision—unless you do it again!

One of the most difficult things about forgiveness is accepting it. God has forgiven you if you asked Him to, but you also have to forgive yourself. Sometimes self-forgiveness can take time. I know in my experience, I've had to ask God every day to help me surrender to Him my guilt from my particular sin. I would ask Him to take the regret from me and to help me to grow beyond it. Anytime regret or guilt enters my mind, I ask Him to take it from me. Eventually, you don't have to ask so often, but it takes dedication to change. You should also consider reaching out to a trusted sister or brother in Christ. Sharing the burden can be a huge relief and an important step toward healing.

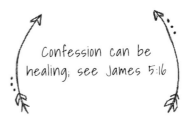

Confession can be healing; see James 5:16

Our God is a God of grace and freedom. Christ wants to free you! (See Galatians 5:1!)

Appendix C

Healing and Forgiving After Abuse

Maybe you have been hurt by someone, like I was when I was 12. Statistics show that a approximately 1 in 7 girls have been sexually abused by their eighteenth birthday. And the really sad part is that in 90% of these cases, the abuse is from someone the victim knows and trusts.

We have only mentioned sexual abuse in this book, but there are many other forms of abuse that we know you or a friend could be facing. God created the family to be a safe place for children to learn and grow. But in this fallen world, many of us come from broken homes, and more and more are growing up in the foster care system. Without the protection that a loving, whole family provides, many children have experienced trauma that is unimaginable.

Those who have been abused in one way or another usually deal with the abuse in one of these ways: they seek love and attention from anyone who will give it to them, they try to hide or ignore the abuse, and they blame themselves for the abuse.

Please hear this truth, from someone who has experienced abuse and all the consequences that go with it: IT IS NOT YOUR FAULT! Nothing justifies abuse.

If something has happened to you, I want to encourage you to remember that secrets only make things worse. God isn't about secrets! Instead, He wants His people to share the burdens that are too much for them to bear. There is freedom in seeking help,

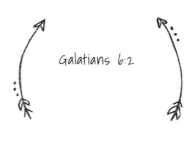

Galatians 6:2

and opening up to someone about what you have experienced or are experiencing.

In addition to sharing your burden with a trusted brother or sister in Christ, I encourage you to seek Christ Himself. If you are looking to heal yourself by seeking love, we want to remind you that the healing you are seeking can only be found in Christ. People of this world will let you down, but Jesus never will. Reach out to Him.

If you need to talk to someone, but would like to do so anonymously, you can call this abuse hotline anytime: 1-866-FOR-LIGHT or text LIGHT to 741741. Trained crisis counselors are available to talk 24/7 for free. All conversations are confidential.

Appendix D

Suffering, But Not Despairing

Have you ever felt truly alone? Maybe so alone that you have gotten to the point of wanting to give up? Have you maybe been the brunt of bullying? That is not okay. We do not want you to feel this way, and we want you to know that there is hope!

Technology gives us access to so much of people's lives. We have more "friends" than ever before. However, today's youth seem to be the least relational generation yet. Social media makes it easy to chat without having to be face to face, which can be great! Social media can be used for a good purpose. But it can also make us feel connected, when in reality, we have tons of friends, but no one to truly listen. Our posts could get a hundred likes, loves, and laughs, but we still feel alone. Social media can be simply a mask we wear, rather than a tool to draw us closer. When God made Adam, He saw that it was not good for men to be alone, so He gave Adam a helper in Eve, and eventually, a family. Today, He also gives us the church, in which we are "members of one another" (Romans 12:4 – 5). We were designed to be in community and real relationship with others! Within a loving group of His people who share with and care for one another, God often unlocks some of His greatest blessings for us.

I encourage you, if you are feeling alone, I mean really alone, reach out to someone.

I have seen more and more teenagers your age choosing to end their lives because of the pain they are experiencing. This is not how life is meant to be. Get involved in your youth group, find someone you trust and share with them what you are experiencing. And PRAY - develop a relationship with God.

When we have faith in God, we know we are created on purpose and for a purpose. Whether we fit in or not, whether we are in the popular crowd or not, no matter what comes our way, we can find encouragement knowing that God made us just how He wants us.

Maybe you do not feel like you have a friend, or anywhere to turn, or maybe this whole God thing is still new to you and a little uncomfortable. I encourage you to keep praying and seeking God in His Word and people among the church. If you'd like to talk to someone anonymously, you can also call 800-273-8255 or text ANSWER to 839863.

And know you can reach out to us. We will pray for you! We do not want you to feel alone! Email us at worthit@p31fitness.com. We want you to know that YOU ARE WORTH IT! God made you on purpose. Do NOT give up!

Would you like to know more about what P31 Fitness has to offer?

P31 Fitness Classes

We offer women-only, faith-based workout classes, based on the Proverbs 31 woman. We focus on all 4 parts of health: Physical, Mental, Emotional and Spiritual.

The workouts offer variety in style, routine, and format and are for women only. Class sessions include cardiovascular work, weight training, kickboxing, body resistance training, stretching, and core work. The workouts will always offer a wide range of variety, so expect something new each time.

We close each class with time to reflect on your spiritual and physical health through a daily devotional, and always have opportunity to share with other women.

Each of the P31 trainers work to ensure safety and proper technique while challenging your body to reach new levels of fitness.

We have classes all over Texas and in surrounding states. We hope to spread all across America! If you would like to see a class in our town - visit our website and contact us! www.p31fitness.com

Become a Trainer

P31 Fitness is looking for enthusiastic women who want to share the gift of health with other women! Do you believe that spirituality is a component of health? Do you want to help women see their worth? Do you LOVE to workout? Do you want to work a few hours a week and earn money doing what you love? P31 Fitness may have the solution for YOU! If you or someone you know is interested in joining the P31 Fitness team, please fill out the Trainer Opportunity Form at p31fitness.com to learn more about becoming a Certified P31 Fitness Trainer.

Become a Franchise Owner

At P31 Fitness we assist woman in achieving balance with home life and commitment to growing in their walk with the Lord. P31 Fitness is about empowering women of all ages and levels of fitness to experience mental, emotional, physical and spiritual freedom through our unique fitness program. If you are looking for a unique, life-changing, faith-based business, then a P31 Fitness franchise could be the perfect fit! Fill out a franchise interest form on our website to see if becoming a P31 Fitness Franchise owner is right for you!! www.p31fitness.com

Young Girls Bootcamp

This bootcamp is designed for upper-elementary-aged girls. The topics covered are similar to those in this book, but geared more toward their age. There is a time for crafts, snacks, and an age-appropriate workout. It is designed to run as three-hour, five-day camp, similar to a Vacation Bible School. They also receive a workbook/bible study book and a shirt during this camp. For more information about this bootcamp, email info@p31fitness.com.

Other resources and books from P31 Fitness

- *Power Your Day with the Power of 4: P31 Fitness Daily Devotionals by Rachel Curtis*
- *Listen and Lose Workbook: My Personal Journey to Spiritual, Physical, Mental and Emotional Health Workbook*
- *Real Recipes, Real Women, Real Results: Recipes for Your Healthy Lifestyle by P31 Fitness*

- *Nutritional consults available through our program to help with the daily meal planning, choices and more. Contact us at info@ p31fitness.com*

Co-authors

 **Larissa Baker** came to know the Lord at a young age and felt the calling to be a teacher. She loves children and worked in public education for seven years before coming home to raise her daughter. She married her high school sweetheart, who serves in the United States Air Force and enjoys supporting him in his career as well as living in the new places the military sends them. Together they have served in different capacities, including student ministry, in their home churches. Although she moves every few years, Texas is home and she goes back as often as she can. She has one daughter and two fur babies at home.

Larissa has been P31 member since May 2016 and a trainer since August 2016. She has always enjoyed fitness and loves how P31 Fitness encompasses all four areas of health: physical, mental, emotional and spiritual. She has experienced freedom and grace through this program and hopes for as many women as possible to experience it as well.

 **Sherri Van Fleet** has known God since she was nine, but really fell in love with Jesus during her high school years. Loving her youth group so much, once she graduated, she became a youth leader herself. Serving as a youth leader led her to meeting her husband, Michael, and settling into her home church in Tucson, AZ. After ten years of youth ministry, she moved into other teaching and service capacities at her church. She has two kids, a boy and a girl, whom she currently homeschools.

Sherri has been a P31 Fitness member since June 2016 and a trainer since March 2017. She has been blessed by this amazing program and hopes for it to reach as many women as possible with God's truth. She considers it a privilege to have been a part of this important project.

Stephanie Gugelman grew up as a churchgoer in a military home, which kept her family moving during her childhood. She didn't know much about the Bible or really understand how to be a Christ-follower, other than to "be a good person." As she shares in this book, something happened in her life that caused her to get really involved in her youth group. There, she accepted Christ as her Lord and Savior. This was a pivotal point in her life.

Another pivotal moment was when Stephanie met her best friend and husband William at Northern Arizona University in 2005. During their first three years of marriage, they moved all over the country seven times because of his job as an Air Force pilot. They have since settled down in Tucson, Arizona, with their three sons.

During these moves, Stephanie not only became a mom, but she also finished her college degree through Northern Arizona University, began a career in personal training, wellness coaching and teaching group fitness classes. She has been leading fitness classes since 2006. Fitness and nutrition have always fascinated her. At one point she even felt as though health had become an unhealthy obsession. She came across P31 Fitness at a time in her life when she felt God convicting her of her priorities, and she immediately knew that God had led her to this program. It encompassed everything she was passionate about: fitness, nutrition and God. Although she was worried about the spiritual part, as she didn't feel equipped to teach it, she knew that God had orchestrated it all! Stephanie is the first to say that her life is an example of God using the least likely for His purpose.

Stephanie began to pursue this dream of getting P31 Fitness started in Arizona in 2015. She first began as a P31 Fitness Trainer, but is now a P31 Fitness Franchise Owner as well. Little did Stephanie know what a dramatic impact this program would have on her life. To this day, she believes that God has her in P31 Fitness for HER! She has experienced so much freedom through it. She was once the girl who would step on the scale two or three times per day deciding what she "could" eat. You can often hear her saying that "the truths we teach our ladies are exactly what I need to be working on myself." She desperately needs the daily reminders of her worth being found in Christ alone, and she believes most women do.

Her mission is to help women and young girls everywhere experience the same freedom and courage that she has, by escaping the bondage of unhealthy self-image and the world's idea of worth. She is still working daily at learning more about the Bible and living the truths she teaches the ladies in her P31 classes. She will be forever grateful for P31 Fitness and she is so honored to have been asked to manage this project and be used by God to bring it to you.

Editor

Kim Mauck gave her life to the Lord at age 12, during a summer "gospel meeting" at the small-town church where she grew up attending. She is so thankful that this was a church where kids were expected to sit quietly during every service, phones were attached to the wall, not your hand, and tablets were something you wrote in, not tapped. All of that meant that she soaked up a lot of Bible without having to do much.

The tough part, for her, then, is not knowing the truth, but *doing* it out of fervent love for God and others. She has to re-learn this daily as a wife, mother of four girls, and college English instructor in small-town Oklahoma.

Contributor

Hillary Grigel is a wife, Mother, MOPS Leader, University of Arizona Alumnus, Architect, speaker, blogger, P31 Member, and sexual assault survivor. These are all titles that can be used to describe Hillary Grigel, yet none as important as: beloved child of God. Hillary feels passionately that we are not defined by past hurts or struggles, but by our identity in Christ. There is nothing God cannot redeem. God answers prayers. God is still in the business of doing miracles. Hillary had the privilege of sharing her message of empowerment, worth and identity in Christ to a P31 Girls Bootcamp, which inspired content in this book. You can learn more about Hillary and her passion for freedom in Christ at: hillarygrigel.com

Artist

Brenda Cicchini is a firstborn, organized planner who has learned over the years that God has plans of his own. She earned a mechanical engineering degree and worked in the defense industry for eight years before making the switch to stay-at-home mom. Now with two kids she spends her days in the kitchen or being creative—often with Play Doh or Legos.

Brenda has been a member of P31 since 2016 and considers it a great honor to be part of this unique project. After a big move turned her life upside down she realized even more there is only one place you can find your true worth—in Christ. She is passionate about sharing the love and kindness of Christ and helping women find hope and security in Jesus.

Made in the USA
Coppell, TX
24 September 2021

62906823R00083

Scriptural Affirmations of Your Worth in His Eyes

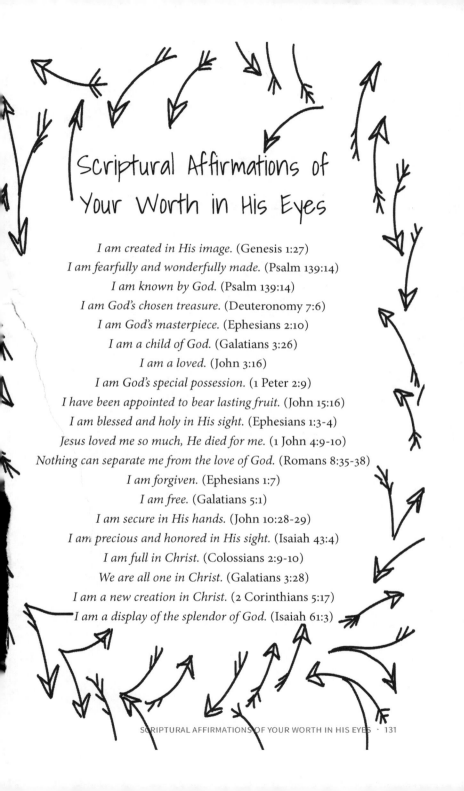

I am created in His image. (Genesis 1:27)
I am fearfully and wonderfully made. (Psalm 139:14)
I am known by God. (Psalm 139:14)
I am God's chosen treasure. (Deuteronomy 7:6)
I am God's masterpiece. (Ephesians 2:10)
I am a child of God. (Galatians 3:26)
I am a loved. (John 3:16)
I am God's special possession. (1 Peter 2:9)
I have been appointed to bear lasting fruit. (John 15:16)
I am blessed and holy in His sight. (Ephesians 1:3-4)
Jesus loved me so much, He died for me. (1 John 4:9-10)
Nothing can separate me from the love of God. (Romans 8:35-38)
I am forgiven. (Ephesians 1:7)
I am free. (Galatians 5:1)
I am secure in His hands. (John 10:28-29)
I am precious and honored in His sight. (Isaiah 43:4)
I am full in Christ. (Colossians 2:9-10)
We are all one in Christ. (Galatians 3:28)
I am a new creation in Christ. (2 Corinthians 5:17)
I am a display of the splendor of God. (Isaiah 61:3)

Appendix B